Lent With St. Francis

DAILY REFLECTIONS

Diane M. Houdek

Franciscan
MEDIA
Cincinnati, Ohio

Cover and book design by Mark Sullivan
Cover image © Fotolia | Zatletic

Library of Congress Cataloging-in-Publication Data

Houdek, Diane M.

Lent with St. Francis : daily reflections / Diane M. Houdek.

p. cm.

ISBN 978-1-61636-524-0 (alk. paper)

1. Lent—Prayers and devotions. 2. Francis, of Assisi, Saint, 1182-1226. I. Title.

BV85.H665 2013

242'.34—dc23

2012035648

ISBN 978-1-61636-524-0

Published by Franciscan Media
28 W. Liberty St.
Cincinnati, OH 45202
www.FranciscanMedia.org

Printed in the United States of America.
Printed on acid-free paper.
13 14 15 16   5 4 3 2

Contents

Introduction | *ix*

Ash Wednesday: *Be Faithful to the Gospel* | *1*
    THURSDAY: *Take Up Your Cross* | *3*
    FRIDAY: *True Fasting* | *5*
    SATURDAY: *We're All Sinners* | *7*

First Week of Lent
    SUNDAY: *Wrestling With Temptation* | *9*
    MONDAY: *The Least of These* | *11*
    TUESDAY: *Our Daily Bread* | *13*
    WEDNESDAY: *Come Follow Me* | *15*
    THURSDAY: *The Gift of Alms* | *17*
    FRIDAY: *Taming the Wolf* | *19*
    SATURDAY: *Francis and the Sultan* | *21*

Second Week of Lent
    SUNDAY: *Ordinary and Extraordinary* | *23*
    MONDAY: *Don't Compare, Don't Judge* | *25*
    TUESDAY: *On Our Own* | *27*
    WEDNESDAY: *True Authority* | *29*
    THURSDAY: *The Money Problem* | *31*

FRIDAY: *Supporting the Church* | 33
SATURDAY: *Giving It All Away* | 35

Third Week of Lent

SUNDAY: *God's Plans for Us* | 37
MONDAY: *True Prophets* | 39
TUESDAY: *Forgive. Then Forgive Again.* | 41
WEDNESDAY: *Cultivate a Peaceful Heart* | 43
THURSDAY: *Nothing to Defend* | 45
FRIDAY: *Perfect Joy* | 47
SATURDAY: *Holy Humility* | 49

Fourth Week of Lent

SUNDAY: *Learning to See* | 51
MONDAY: *Signs and Wonders* | 53
TUESDAY: *Do We Like Complaining?* | 55
WEDNESDAY: *The Virtue of Work* | 57
THURSDAY: *How Do Others See Us?* | 59
FRIDAY: *The Kingdom Is Right Here* | 61
SATURDAY: *Limitations* | 63

Fifth Week of Lent

SUNDAY: *Sister Death* | 65
MONDAY: *Great Compassion* | 67
TUESDAY: *The Sign of the Cross* | 69

WEDNESDAY: *True Disciples* | 71
THURSDAY: *What Is Ours?* | 73
FRIDAY: *Praising God* | 75
SATURDAY: *Worldly Power* | 77

Holy Week
PALM SUNDAY: *The Cross Is Before Us* | 79
MONDAY: *True Concern for the Poor* | 81
TUESDAY: *Love of Money* | 83
WEDNESDAY: *Betrayal* | 85

Easter Triduum
HOLY THURSDAY: *Eucharist* | 87
GOOD FRIDAY: *"By Your Holy Cross"* | 89
HOLY SATURDAY | EASTER VIGIL: *Dead to Sin* | 91
EASTER SUNDAY: *"Let Us Begin Again"* | 93

Introduction

"Let us begin again, for until now we have done nothing."

Francis spoke these words shortly before his death. Like Jesus leaving the disciples to return to his Father in heaven, Francis wants his followers to hold fast to the rule he established. He's seen something of what is likely to happen to the order after his death. It's not so much a question of pride or ego, not wanting anything he did to change. Rather he recognizes the danger of institutionalizing a charismatic vision.

We always need to find new ways of doing things if we're not going to settle into ruts that will only get us where we've gone before. St. Francis, like so many other saints, recognizes that Jesus's call extends beyond slavish imitation to a living out of the spirit behind the rule.

One reason St. Francis is such a popular example of holiness is that he stayed so close to the Gospel in everything that he did. His imitation of Christ is one that all of us can strive to emulate. Francis lived the teachings of Jesus, often quite literally, from the time of his conversion until his death. In doing so, he inspired people of his own time, as well as millions from his day to our own, to do likewise.

The *Legend of the Three Companions*, one of the early accounts of his life, describes Francis's ministry in this way:

> From this time onward Saint Francis wandered through cities, villages, and hamlets, and began to preach with increasing perfection, not using learned words of human wisdom, but through the doctrine and virtue of the Holy Spirit most confidently proclaiming the kingdom of God. He was a genuine preacher confirmed by apostolic authority; therefore he spoke no honeyed words of flattery or blandishment; what he preached to others he had already put into practice himself and his teaching of the truth was full of assurance. The power and truth of what he said did not come from any human source; and his words impressed many learned and cultured men who hastened to

see and hear him as though he were a being from another century. Many of the people, nobles and commoners alike, were touched by divine inspiration and began to imitate Francis's way of life, and to follow in his steps. They abandoned the cares and pomps of the world, desiring to live under his direction, guidance, and discipline.

People responded to Francis in ways that nothing he said or did can adequately explain. Even one of his closest followers, Brother Masseo, asked him once, "Why after you? Why does everyone follow after you?"

Francis had a certain charisma, but he didn't like being a leader and wasn't looking for followers, just companions. The simplicity of his lifestyle may have been attractive to some, but in his day as in ours a lavish lifestyle was always more desirable than the subsistence living of the "little poor man."

In following Francis, people knew they were following Christ. It's no accident that the cross is at the center of the lives of both Jesus and Francis. It is the ultimate symbol of letting go of everything that gets in the way of a life lived for God and God alone. The power of that sign is unmistakable.

Francis lived in a singularly Catholic culture, one we can hardly imagine in our global village and its diversity of religious belief—including no belief at all.

In the thirteenth century, the Protestant Reformation was hundreds of years in the future. Nevertheless, there were frequent disputes over questions of doctrine and ever-present problems of heresy. The papacy itself would be endangered by claims and counterclaims to the papal throne. The Church of Francis's day was involved in political struggles and even wars, including the Crusades and local territorial conflicts.

Francis, from the time of his conversion, threaded a path through these troublesome issues by searching the Gospels and the prayer and liturgy of the Church for a way to live what he had always believed. He took seriously the Gospel command to choose poverty and service over power and prestige, to love one's enemies, to place love of God before any earthly desires.

As we follow Francis through this Lenten season, we can rely on his inspiration to conform our lives more closely to the pattern of the Gospels.

Ash Wednesday
BE FAITHFUL TO THE GOSPEL
Joel 2:12–18; Psalm 51:3–4, 5–6, 12–13, 17;
2 Corinthians 5:20—6:2; Matthew 6:1–6, 16–18

"Turn away from sin and be faithful to the Gospel."

These are the words most often used as we are signed with ashes. It is a call to conversion, a call to follow Christ, a call to change our lives. Today's reading from the Gospel of Matthew gives us the three pillars of Lent—prayer, fasting, and almsgiving. These are at the heart of the Gospel's message. No one heard this call and followed it more devotedly than St. Francis of Assisi.

But when on a certain day the Gospel was read in [the church of the Portiuncula] how the Lord sent his disciples out to preach, the holy man of God, assisting there, understood somewhat the words of the Gospel; after Mass he humbly asked the priest to explain the Gospel to him more fully. When he had set forth for him in order all these things, the holy Francis, hearing that the disciples of Christ should not possess gold or silver or money; nor carry along the way scrip, or wallet, or bread, or a staff; that they should not have shoes, or two tunics; but that they should preach the kingdom of God and penance, immediately cried out exultingly: "This is what I wish, this is what I seek, this is what I long to do with all my heart."

Francis took a literal approach to the Gospel. He began with the most basic interpretation of a text, but he didn't stop there. He began by throwing aside his tunic, shoes, and walking staff, but over time discovered the many ways in which possessions can keep us from seeking God. He began by carrying stones and fitting them into the crumbling walls of Assisi's churches, but over time he inspired his followers to reinvigorate the Church with the undimmed power of the Gospel.

Prayer

Most High, Glorious God,
bring light to the darkness of my heart,
give me right faith, certain hope, and perfect charity.
Lord, give me insight and wisdom
so I might always discern
your holy and true will.
Amen.

Thursday After Ash Wednesday
TAKE UP YOUR CROSS
Deuteronomy 30:15–20; Psalm 1:1–2, 3–4, 6;
Luke 9:22–25

"If any want to become my followers, let them deny themselves and take up their cross daily and follow me."
—Luke 9:23

This is one of the three foundational texts of Francis's rule of life. When Bernard of Quintavalle told Francis he wanted to join his life of poverty, they spoke to the parish priest and, under his guidance, opened the Scriptures three times, a common practice in medieval times. The three passages they read that day eventually became part of Francis's Rule:

The Rule and life of the friars is to live in obedience, in chastity and without property, following the teaching and the footsteps of our Lord Jesus Christ who says, If thou wilt be perfect, go, sell what thou hast, and give to the poor, and thou shalt have treasure in heaven; and come, follow me (Matthew 19:21); and, If anyone wishes to come after me, let him deny himself, and take up his cross, and follow me (Matthew 16:24). Elsewhere he says, If anyone comes to me and does not hate his father and mother, and wife and children, and brothers and sisters, yes, and even his own life, he cannot be my disciple (Luke 14:26). And everyone who has left house, or brothers, or sisters, or father, or mother, or wife, or children, or lands, for my name's sake, shall receive a hundredfold, and shall possess life everlasting (Matthew 19:29).

These passages express the need to put Christ at the center of all we think, say, and do. If our own goals, possessions, and even families and friends distract us from the Lord's call, then we are not truly choosing life. In an ideal world, all these things should bring us closer to God—and we should bring them closer to God.

Prayer

We adore you, Lord Jesus Christ,
here and in all your churches
in the whole world,
and we bless you,
because by your holy cross
you have redeemed the world.
Amen.

Friday After Ash Wednesday
TRUE FASTING
Isaiah 58:1–9a; Psalm 51:3–4, 5–6ab, 18–19;
Matthew 9:14–15

Is not this the fast that I choose:
   to loose the bonds of injustice,
   to undo the thongs of the yoke,
to let the oppressed go free,
   and to break every yoke?
Is it not to share your bread with the hungry,
   and bring the homeless poor into your house.
               —Isaiah 58:6–7

An early follower of Francis was not able to sustain the extreme fasting that Francis himself practiced. Rather than shaming the man, Francis broke his own fast so that his hungry brother could eat.

He commanded the table to be set, though it was filled with poor things, and, as is often the case, where wine was lacking water took its place. First he himself began to eat, and then he invited the rest of the brothers to share this duty of charity, lest that brother should waste away from shame.... He

5

said that to deprive the body indiscreetly of what it needs was a sin just the same as it is a sin to give it superfluous things at the prompting of gluttony. And he added: "Know, dearest brothers, that what I have done in eating, I have done by dispensation, not by desire, because fraternal charity commanded it."

Religious practices can never become more important than the end to which they lead: love of God and love of neighbor. Jesus makes this point again and again in the Gospels. It's a good lesson at the beginning of Lent. *What* we do for Lent is far less important than *why* we do it. The time-honored traditions of prayer, fasting, and almsgiving are less to benefit us than to draw us closer to God and improve the lives of those around us.

Prayer

Almighty, most high and supreme God, Father, holy and just, Lord, King of heaven and earth, we give you thanks for yourself. Of your own holy will you created all things spiritual and physical, made us in your own image and likeness, and gave us a place in paradise, through your only Son, in the Holy Spirit. Amen.

Saturday After Ash Wednesday
We're All Sinners
Isaiah 58:9b–14; Psalm 86:1–2, 3–4, 5–6; Luke 5:27–32

"Those who are well have no need of a physician, but those who are sick; I have come to call not the righteous but sinners to repentance."

—Luke 5:31–32

Francis used this passage from Scripture to rebuke the guardian of one of the houses where the brothers were living. The guardian had driven away a band of thieves from the house and proudly told Francis of his deed.

St. Francis scolded him severely, saying: "You acted in a cruel way, because sinners are led back to God by holy meekness better than by cruel scolding. For our Master Jesus Christ, whose Gospel we have promised to observe, says that the doctor is not needed by those who are well but by the sick, and 'I have come to call not the just but sinners to penance,' and therefore He often ate with them. So, since you acted against charity and against the example of Jesus Christ, I order you under holy obedience to take right now this sack of bread and jug of wine which I begged. Go and look carefully for those robbers over the mountains and valleys until you find them. And offer them all this bread and this wine for me. And then kneel down before them and humbly accuse yourself of your sin of cruelty.

We find it difficult to admit when we're wrong, when we've sinned. And it seems the more we try to live good Christian lives, the harder it gets to acknowledge how often we fail.

It is that acknowledgment, though, that allows us to find the forgiveness and grace we need to change our lives.

Prayer

We give you thanks because, having created us through your Son, by that holy love with which you loved us, you decreed that he should be born, true God and true man, of the glorious and ever blessed Virgin Mary and redeem us from our captivity by the blood of his passion and death. Amen.

First Sunday of Lent
WRESTLING WITH TEMPTATION

Year A: Genesis 2:7–9, 3:1–7; Psalm 51:3–4, 5–6,
12–13, 17; Romans 5:12–19; Matthew 4:1–11
Year B: Genesis 9:8–15; Psalm 25:4–5, 6–7, 8–9; 1
Peter 3:18–22; Mark 1:12–15
Year C: Deuteronomy 26:4–10; Psalm 91:1–2, 10–11,
12–13, 14–15; Romans 10:8–13; Luke 4:1–13

"Jesus, full of the Holy Spirit, returned from the
Jordan and was led by the Spirit in the wilder-
ness, where for forty days he was tempted by the
devil."

—Luke 4:1

Our temptations aren't likely to come to us from a
mysterious figure in a deserted place. But often they
revolve around the same basic human drives: hunger,
emotional security, safety, status, ambition.

Many of the stories told about St. Francis reveal his
struggles with temptations of various kinds, as in this
story, from the *Legend of the Three Companions*:

When the Devil saw Francis's good beginning, he
tried ingeniously to turn him from it by suggestions

of fright or disgust…. Francis, however, was strong in the Lord and, heedless of the Devil's threats, he prayed devoutly in the cave that God would direct his steps into the right way.

The message of the Gospel today, like the message of Lent itself, is twofold: "Repent and believe the good news." We are called to do both. It's easy to think that the repenting is the hard part. But in all honesty, often it's far more difficult to believe in good news. We know our weaknesses far better than we know our strengths.

Prayer

Almighty, eternal, just and merciful God, grant us in our misery that we may do for your sake alone what we know you want us to do, and always want what pleases you; so that, cleansed and enlightened interiorly and fired with the ardour of the Holy Spirit, we may be able to follow in the footsteps of your Son, our Lord Jesus Christ. Amen.

Monday of the First Week of Lent
THE LEAST OF THESE
Leviticus 19:1–2, 11–18; Psalm 19:8, 9, 10, 15;
Matthew 25:31–46

"Truly I tell you, just as you did it to one of the least of these who are members of my family, you did it to me."

—Matthew 25:40

If we followed only this verse in the Gospel, we would understand and be part of the kingdom of God. Francis spent his entire life after his conversion serving the least and the lowly. In doing so, he came to know Jesus.

From the time he spontaneously embraced the leper, after so many years of being repulsed at the very sight of lepers on the outskirts of Assisi, he recognized the presence of Christ in everyone he met.

Francis knew that he needed to confront something deep within his soul that was keeping him from following Christ. We might pause to ask what fear we need to confront.

In his last written words to his brothers, his *Testament*, Francis said:

This is how God inspired me, Brother Francis, to embark upon a life of penance. When I was in sin, the sight of lepers nauseated me beyond measure; but then God himself led me into their company, and I had pity on them. When I had once become acquainted with them, what had previously nauseated me became a source of spiritual and physical consolation for me. After that I did not wait long before leaving the world.

Prayer

We should wish for nothing else and have no other desire; we should find no pleasure or delight in anything except in our Creator, Redeemer, and Saviour; he alone is true God, who is perfect good, all good, every good. Amen.

Tuesday of the First Week of Lent
OUR DAILY BREAD
Isaiah 55:10–11; Psalm 34:4–5, 6–7, 16–17, 18–19;
Matthew 6:7–15

"Your Father knows what you need before you ask him."

—Matthew 6:7

In committing himself to a life of poverty, Francis took seriously the belief that God would provide his daily bread. He was also mindful of the impression he and his brothers made, leaving their wealth and then begging food from the townspeople.

When they begged for alms in the city they received very little else than reproaches at having left their own possessions in order to eat at the expense of others. This caused them much suffering and great want. They were persecuted by their friends and relatives and by the citizens generally, both rich and poor, of all ranks, who derided them as madmen and fools, because at that time no one spontaneously left his own goods to beg from door to door.

Francis began his new life by rebuilding churches stone by stone. He and his early followers offered to work in the fields around Assisi in return for food and a place to sleep. With Jesus, he believed that "a laborer is worthy of his hire" (Luke 10:7). If they couldn't find work, they would beg what they needed for that day.

Our world is far different than that of a medieval walled city, but the basic principles remain the same. We need to be mindful of those who seek work, but also of those who need basic food and shelter.

Prayer

Nothing, then, must keep us back, nothing separate us from him, nothing come between us and him. At all times and seasons, in every country and place, every day and all day, we must have a true and humble faith, and keep him in our hearts. Amen.

Wednesday of the First Week of Lent
COME FOLLOW ME

Jonah 3:1–10; Psalm 51:3–4, 12–13, 18–19;
Luke 11:29–32

"This generation is an evil generation; it asks for a sign, but no sign will be given to it except the sign of Jonah."

—Luke 11:29

Jonah was the stereotypical doomsday prophet, proclaiming, "The end is near. Repent!" Francis stood out from the crowd, too. Assuredly there were many who ignored or ridiculed him. But he was extraordinarily effective in getting people to follow him, a charismatic attraction that continues to our own day. The sincerity with which he lived his faith must have had a great deal to do with that.

The truth of his teaching was brought home to people by the simplicity of his way of life, and two years after his own conversion several men were drawn to follow his example of penitence, and they left everything in order to join him. The first of these was Brother Bernard of holy memory. He well knew how luxuriously Francis had lived in the world; therefore, when he saw how he labored to restore ruined churches and what a harsh life he led, Bernard too resolved to sell his possessions and give all to the poor. It seemed to him the will of God that he should follow Francis in clothing and his whole manner of life. With this in mind he went one day secretly to see God's servant and opened his heart to him, also inviting him to come that evening and lodge in his house.

Not all of us are called to give dramatic, public witness to God's word. We are all called, however, to live the Gospel in our lives.

Prayer

With all our hearts and all our souls, all our minds and all our strength, all our power and all our understanding, with every faculty (see Deuteronomy 6:5) and every effort, with every affection and all our emotions, with every wish and desire, we should love our Lord and God who has given and gives us everything, body and soul, and all our life. Amen.

Thursday of the First Week of Lent
THE GIFT OF ALMS
Esther C:12, 14–16, 23–25; Psalm 138:1–2ab,
2cde–3, 7c–8; Matthew 7:7–12

"If you then, who are evil, know how to give good gifts to your children, how much more will your Father in heaven give good things to those who ask him!"

—Matthew 7:11

With passages such as we find in today's Gospel, it's not hard to see how Francis decided that relying on other people to provide for the brothers' needs was a way of living out their total reliance on God.

Once when St. Francis visited [Cardinal Hugolino], and the hour of dinner was at hand, he went out for alms, and returning, placed some of the scraps of black bread on the bishop's table.... When the dinner was finished, the bishop arose and taking the man of God to an inner room, he raised his arms and embraced him. "My Brother," he said, "why did you bring shame on me in the house that is yours and your brothers by going out for alms?" The saint said to him: "Rather I have shown you honor, for I have honored a greater lord. For the Lord is well pleased with poverty, and above all with that poverty that is voluntary. For I have a royal dignity and a special nobility, namely, to follow the Lord who, being rich, became poor for us." And he added: "I get more delight from a poor table that is furnished with small alms than from great tables on which dainty foods are placed almost without number." Then, greatly edified, the bishop said to the saint: "Son, do what seems good in your eyes, for the Lord is with you."

It is hard to depend on other people. We feel ashamed when we are in need and in turn shame those who need help from others, especially if they are "undeserving." Francis teaches us that by learning to rely on the Lord and on the gifts we receive from others—and all is gift—we are as needy as any beggar on the street.

Prayer

You are all our riches,
And you suffice for us.
Amen.

Friday of the First Week of Lent
TAMING THE WOLF
Ezekiel 18:21–28; Psalm 130:1–2, 3–4, 5–7a,
7bc–8; Matthew 5:20–26

"When the wicked turn away from the wickedness they have committed and do what is lawful and right, they shall save their life."

—Ezekiel 18:27

One of the best-known stories of St. Francis is that of his taming the fierce wolf of Gubbio. Francis speaks to the wolf that has been terrorizing the town. He addresses him from the beginning as "Brother Wolf" and so acknowledges a connection with the creature. He asks the wolf to agree to stop murdering the townspeople. Then he uses the opportunity to preach to the people about their own need for penance and forgiveness.

"So, dear people," he said, "come back to the Lord, and do fitting penance, and God will free you from the wolf in this world and from the devouring fire of hell in the next world." And having said that, he added: "Listen, dear people. Brother Wolf, who is standing here before you, has promised me and has given me a pledge that he will make peace with you and will never hurt you if you promise also to feed him every day. And I pledge myself as bondsman for Brother Wolf that he will faithfully keep this peace pact."

Jesus and Francis both know that often the evil that we see and hate in others reflects some shadowy part of our own attitudes, thoughts, and behaviors. The wolf of Gubbio is a reminder to us that we need to confront our fears and anger, taming them with the love of God.

Prayer

Holy Obedience puts to shame all natural and selfish desires.

It mortifies our lower nature and makes it obey the spirit and our fellow men.

Obedience subjects a man to everyone on earth,

And not only to men,

but to all the beasts as well and to the wild animals,

So that they can do what they like with him, as far as God allows them.

Amen.

Saturday of the First Week of Lent
FRANCIS AND THE SULTAN
Deuteronomy 26:16–19; Psalm 119:1–2, 4–5, 7–8;
Matthew 5:43–48

"Love your enemies, and pray for those who perse-
cute you."

—Matthew 5:44

The best illustration from the life of Francis of his willingness to take this passage seriously was his journey to
visit the sultan. The Crusades were still in full swing at
this time. Francis's willingness to meet with and talk to
the sultan showed a level of tolerance that few of his
day could match, although Sultan Malik al-Kamil was
himself known for his tolerance of other faiths. They
were well-matched for this meeting.

The sultan honored him as much as he was able,
and having given him many gifts, he tried to bend
Francis's mind toward the riches of the world. But
when he saw that Francis most vigorously despised
all these things as so much dung, he was filled with
the greatest admiration, and he looked upon him
as a man different from all others. He was deeply

moved by his words and he listened to him very willingly.

This meeting between Francis and the sultan has received a great deal of attention in our own century. The need for peace and understanding is as great in our time as it was during the Crusades, and sometimes as little valued. Francis still sets an example for us. And Jesus's command still holds true.

Prayer

O Divine Master,

grant that I may not so much seek to be consoled, as to console;

to be understood, as to understand;

to be loved, as to love.

For it is in giving that we receive.

It is in pardoning that we are pardoned,

and it is in dying that we are born to Eternal Life.

Amen.

Second Sunday of Lent
ORDINARY AND EXTRAORDINARY

Year A: Genesis 12:1–4a; Psalm 33:4–5, 18–19, 20, 22;
2 Timothy 1:8–10; Matthew 17:1–9
Year B: Genesis 22:1–2, 9a, 10–13, 15–18;
Psalm 116:10, 15, 16–17, 18–19;
Romans 8:31b–34; Mark 9:2–10
Year C: Genesis 15:5–12, 17–18; Psalm 27:1, 7–8a,
8b–9, 13–14; Philippians 3:17—4:1;
Luke 9:28b–36

"And while he was praying, the appearance of his face changed, and his clothes became dazzling white."

—Luke 9:29

The transfiguration was an extraordinary moment. Such moments don't happen very often. But when they do, they change everything.

Perhaps the greatest experience of Francis's life took place on Mount La Verna. Having prayed long and hard to share in the sufferings of Christ crucified, he had a vision of a six-winged seraph and of Jesus on the cross. He received the marks of the nails in his hands and feet, as well as the gash left by the spear that pierced Jesus's side. But he was careful to keep the wounds hidden. Francis didn't want to call attention to his experience in a way that would sensationalize it. Francis understood that the essential message of living a Gospel life was to follow in the footsteps of Jesus.

For most of us, the extraordinary experiences are hidden in something quite ordinary. A job opportunity takes us someplace we never imagined we would be, and our experiences there change us immeasurably. Or we meet someone who brings us to a completely new awareness of the power of faith in our everyday activities. We don't need to go looking for extraordinary, mountaintop experiences.

Prayer

We are all poor sinners and unworthy even to mention your name, and so we beg our Lord Jesus Christ, your beloved Son, in whom you are well pleased (Matthew 17:5)…; there is never anything lacking in him to accomplish your will, and it is through him that you have done so much for us. Amen.

Monday of the Second Week of Lent
Don't Compare, Don't Judge
Daniel 9:4b–10; Psalm 79:8, 9, 11, 13; Luke 6:36–38

"Do not judge, and you will not be judged; do not condemn, and you will not be condemned. Forgive, and you will be forgiven; give, and it will be given to you."

—Luke 6:37–38

Jesus reserved his harshest words in the Gospels for those who thought they were spiritually superior to others. Francis, too, recognized that this failing threatened those who had given up everything to follow him in his Gospel commitment to a life of poverty, prayer, and penance.

He emphasized to his followers that they were to examine their own lives rather than pointing fingers at others. He said in his Rule of 1223: "I warn all the friars and exhort them not to condemn or look down on people whom they see wearing soft or gaudy clothes and enjoying luxuries in food or drink; each one should rather condemn and despise himself."

We will always encounter people who are better than we are and worse than we are on nearly every human, social, and spiritual level. If we begin making comparisons, soon we will be making judgments, about them and about ourselves. In doing so, we quickly lose sight of who we are: unique individuals created and loved by God for ourselves, not on some cosmic grading curve.

Prayer

Where there is Poverty and Joy, there is neither Cupidity nor Avarice.

Where there is Peace and Contemplation, there is neither Care nor Restlessness.

Amen.

Tuesday of the Second Week of Lent
On Our Own
Isaiah 1:10, 16–20; Psalm 50:8–9, 16bc–17, 21, 23;
Matthew 23:1–12

"And call no one your father on earth, for you have one Father—the one in heaven."

—Matthew 23:9

One of the iconic moments in Francis's life was when he stood before the bishop and people of Assisi stripped not only of the clothing that belonged to his father, but of his very identity as his father's son.

> Thereupon the servant of God rose joyfully…and holding out the money, he said: "My Lord Bishop, not only will I gladly give back the money which is my father's, but also my clothes." Going into the Bishop's room he stripped himself of his garments and placing the money on them he stood naked before the eyes of the Bishop, his father, and all present and said: "…Hitherto I have called Peter Bernardone my father; but because I am resolved to serve God I return to him the money on account of which he was so perturbed, and also the clothes

I wore which are his; and from now on I will say 'Our Father who art in heaven,' and not Father Peter Bernardone."

At some point, most of us have to stand up for ourselves apart from our parents, our siblings, our friends. While we share many things in common, we also have our own ideas and ways of doing things. We may not have as drastic a break as Francis and Pietro, but we still become our own persons as we mature. This prepares us to one day stand before God and account for our lives as we have lived them, not blaming anyone for our failures.

Prayer

Our Father, who art in heaven,
hallowed be your name.
Your kingdom come, your will be done, on earth as
  it is in heaven.
Give us this day our daily bread,
and forgive us our trespasses as we forgive those who
  trespass against us.
Lead us not into temptation,
but deliver us from evil. Amen.

Wednesday of the Second Week of Lent
TRUE AUTHORITY
Jeremiah 18:18–20; Psalm 31:5–6, 14, 15–16; Matthew 20:17–28

"It will not be so among you; but whoever wishes to be great among you must be your servant, and whoever wishes to be first among you must be your slave."

—Matthew 20:26–28

As we see in today's Gospel, Jesus had to deal with his followers jockeying for positions of power. He tries to show them how the Chrisian life must be different from that of the pagan rulers around them—and indeed from some of the religious structures in his tradition.

Francis emphasized this point too, writing it into his Rule and even ceding leadership of his own community to others.

All the friars without exception are forbidden to wield power or authority, particularly over one another. Our Lord tells us in the Gospel that the rulers of the Gentiles lord it over them, and their great men exercise authority over them (Matthew

20:25). That is not to be the way among the friars. Among them whoever wishes to become great shall be their servant, and whoever wishes to be first shall be their minister (Matthew 28:26–28), and he is their servant. Let him who is the greatest among you become as the youngest (Luke 22:26).

Servant leadership continues to be a difficult concept, perhaps because so many business and political organizations elevate power and authority to ends in themselves. Jesus makes it clear that if we follow his way, we need to embrace his model of humility. The best way to do this is to remind ourselves that all power belongs only to God.

Prayer

You are holy, Lord, the only God, and your deeds are
   wonderful.
You are strong.
You are great.
You are the Most High,
You are almighty.
Amen.

Thursday of the Second Week of Lent
THE MONEY PROBLEM
Jeremiah 17:5–10; Psalm 1:1–2, 3, 4, 6;
Luke 16:19–31

"Child, remember that during your lifetime you received your good things, and Lazarus in like manner evil things; but now he is comforted here, and you are in agony."

—Luke 16:25

Built on a hill, the medieval city of Assisi shows how the social divisions between high and low were not merely metaphorical. The nobility lived at the top of the city; the poor people lived at the bottom; the rising merchant class lived in between. And outside the walls, in the swamps and marches, the lepers and other outcasts struggled to stay alive.

One of the defining moments of Francis's conversion, his embrace of the leper, shattered his social aspirations and inspired him not merely to care for the poor and outcast, but to live among them as one of them. His motivation was always his great gratitude that Jesus himself did not cling to his divinity, but became human like us.

Unlike the rich man in today's Gospel, Francis not only noticed the poor at the gate, he did what he could to alleviate their suffering. He heard and heeded the warnings not only of Moses and the prophets, but also of the one who had actually risen from the dead.

The money-based economy that was new and even revolutionary in Francis's day is something we take for granted today. But it never hurts to ask questions about our priorities in light of the Gospel call to sell what we have and give to the poor. We—and our churches— will be better for having done so.

Francis so identified with the poor outside the walls of Assisi that he desired to be buried there. The Basilica of St. Francis stands outside the walls he knew.

Prayer

You are our faith,
Our great consolation.
Amen.

Friday of the Second Week of Lent
SUPPORTING THE CHURCH
Genesis 37:3–4, 12–13a, 17b–28a; Psalm 105:16–17, 18–19,
20–21; Matthew 21:33–43, 45–46

"The stone that the builders rejected
has become the cornerstone."

—Matthew 21:42

Franciscan visitors to the Basilica of St. John Lateran
in Rome take a special delight in a sculpture of Francis,
arms raised, that stands a block or two away. Looking
at the basilica from behind the statue, it appears that
Francis is holding up the church. The inspiration
for this is a story told of Francis and Pope Innocent
III. Francis had traveled to Rome to seek the pope's
approval for this new way of life he wanted to share
with the brothers the Lord had inspired to follow him.

The pope, at first disinclined to grant Francis's
request, had dreamed of just such a person.

He had seen in his sleep the Lateran basilica about
to fall to ruin, when a certain religious, small and
despised, propped it up by putting his own back
under it lest it fall. "Surely," he said, "this is that man

who, by his works and by the teaching of Christ, will give support to the Church." ... Therefore, filled with love of God he always showed a special love toward the servant of Christ. And therefore he quickly granted what had been asked, and he promised to grant even greater things than these.

In spite of his radical commitment to live the Gospel, apart from many of the cultural institutions that had influenced the Church by the thirteenth century, Francis still remained a faithful, obedient son of the Church.

He insisted on having the pope's approval of his Rule, even though he believed that way of life had come to him directly from God. Francis and his followers were committed to supporting and building up the Church, all the while reforming it from within and bringing it always into greater conformation to the Gospel.

Prayer

Happy those who endure in peace,
By you, Most High, they will be crowned.
Amen.

Saturday of the Second Week of Lent
GIVING IT ALL AWAY
Micah 7:14–15, 18–20; Psalm 103:1–2, 3–4,
9–10, 11–12; Luke 15:1–3, 11–32

"I am no longer worthy to be called your son; treat
me like one of your hired hands."

—Luke 15:19

Today's Gospel tells the familiar story of the Prodigal
Son. Many of us can identify with this rebellious
younger son who loses himself in pleasure and adven-
ture. And we also know what it's like to come to our
senses and realize that we've taken a wrong turn.

One of the things that makes Francis's story so
engaging is that his early life seemed far from saintly.
He was a young man of his time and social class.

> Francis grew up quick and clever, and he followed
> in his father's footsteps by becoming a merchant....
> He was a spendthrift, and all that he earned went
> into eating and carousing with his friends. For this
> his parents often remonstrated with him, saying
> that in squandering such large sums on himself
> and others, his style of living made him appear not

so much their son as the son of some great prince. However, being rich and loving him tenderly, they allowed him free rein in order to avoid displeasing him….

Grace, working through these natural virtues, brought him to the point of being able to say to himself: "Since you are courteous and generous to men from whom you only receive vain and transitory favors, it is only fair that you should be equally so to those in need, since the Lord God is magnanimous in repaying whatever is given to his poor." From that time on Francis welcomed the poor and gave them abundant alms.

Those who worry about whether there will be enough find it difficult to give freely. Those accustomed to giving it all away find it easier to accept God's grace.

Prayer

Holy Humility puts pride to shame,
and all the inhabitants of this world and all that is in the world.
Amen.

Third Sunday of Lent
GOD'S PLANS FOR US

Year A: Exodus 17:3–7; Psalm 95:1–2, 6–7, 8–9; Romans
5:1–2, 5–8; John 4:5–42

Year B: Exodus 20:1–17; Psalm 19:8, 9, 10, 11; 1
Corinthians 1:22–25; John 2:13–25

Year C: Exodus 3:1–8a, 13–15; Psalm 103:1–2,
3–4, 6–7, 8, 11; 1 Corinthians 10:1–6, 10–12;
Luke 13:1–9

"Jesus said to them, 'My food is to do the will of
him who sent me and to complete his work.'"
—John 4:34

If we forget everything else in our relationship with
God, we need to remember that we are called into an
unbreakable covenant with the Divine. Whatever our
destiny, we must respond to the Lord's call.

When Francis was in his early twenties, he rode off to
battle against the nearby city-state of Perugia. He was
captured and imprisoned for a year. He returned home
sick and spent the next year virtually bedridden. When
he recovered from his illness, he spent time simply
wandering the area, praying in abandoned chapels,

walking in the woods and on the slopes of Mount Subasio, spending time in caves listening first to the silence and then to the voice of God.

Francis was not the first saint to have encountered God during an illness. There's something about serious illness that forces us to confront our mortality and then to question our priorities. Francis had longed to be a knight, a soldier, to do great deeds on the field of battle. When he lost that opportunity, he had a choice between spending the rest of his life depressed at his ill fortune or listening to the plans God had for him.

Prayer
You are our eternal life,
Great and wonderful Lord,
God almighty,
Merciful Savior.
Amen.

Monday of the Third Week of Lent
TRUE PROPHETS
2 Kings 5:1–15a; Psalm 42:2–3; 43:3–4;
Luke 4:24–30

"And he said, 'Truly I tell you, no prophet is accepted in the prophet's home town.'"

—Luke 4:24

Everyone in Assisi knew Francis Bernardone. Whether he was leading the other young men of the town in nightly revels or leading a small group of Lesser Brothers in prayer and penitence, he couldn't be missed—or ignored. His biographers give us a glimpse into his family's response to his conversion:

When his father saw him in this pitiful plight, he was filled with sorrow, for he had loved him very dearly; he was both grieved and ashamed to see his son half dead from penance and hardships, and whenever they met, he cursed Francis. When the servant of God heard his father's curses, he took as his father a poor and despised outcast and said to him: "Come with me and I will give you the alms I receive; and when I hear my father cursing me, I shall turn to you saying: 'Bless me, Father'; and then you will sign me with the cross and bless me in his place." And when this happened, the beggar did indeed bless him; and Francis turned to his father, saying: "Do you not realize that God can give me a father whose blessing will counter your curses?" Many people, seeing his patience in suffering scorn, were amazed and upheld him admiringly.

We often find it difficult to recognize the true prophets in our midst. We dismiss them as crackpots and extremists because they make us uncomfortable.

Francis might give us the inspiration we need to pause and listen to the people around us and, in their voices, hear the voice of God.

Prayer
The person who practices one virtue and does not
    offend against the others possesses all.
The person who offends against one virtue,
possesses none and violates all.
Amen.

Tuesday of the Third Week of Lent

FORGIVE. THEN FORGIVE AGAIN.

Daniel 3:25, 34–43; Psalm 25:4bc–5ab, 6, 7bc, 8–9;
Matthew 18:21–35

"Lord, if another member of the church sins against me, how often should I forgive?"

—Matthew 18:21

Forgiveness is quite possibly the most difficult and yet essential action necessary for anyone living in community. Unless we're hermits, that includes all of us.

One day two of the brothers came upon a madman who started throwing stones at them; and when one saw a stone aimed at the other he intercepted it, wishing rather to receive the blow himself. Indeed, each was ready to give his life for the other. This and similar things were possible because they were so deeply rooted in mutual love: each one humbly reverenced his brother as a father or mother; and those brothers who held some office, or were distinguished by some special gift appeared the most humble and unpretentious of all....

Each brother studied to oppose any vice with the opposite virtue, helped and guided by the grace of our Lord Jesus Christ. Nothing was considered as private property; any book given to one brother was used by all according to the rule observed and handed down by the Apostles; because the brothers lived in true poverty they were correspondingly generous and openhanded with everything given them for love of God. For love of him they gladly gave to all who asked something of them, and especially they handed on to the poor any alms they received.

Life in community always has its rough spots. But as with the Gospel, the ideal is always there, difficult as it is. We need to hear Jesus's words about forgiveness until we stop asking the question, "How often must I forgive?"

Prayer

Pure and holy Simplicity puts all the learning of this world, all natural wisdom, to shame.

Holy Poverty puts to shame all greed, avarice, and all the anxieties of this life. Amen.

Wednesday of the Third Week of Lent
CULTIVATE A PEACEFUL HEART
Deuteronomy 4:1, 5–9; Psalm 147:12–13, 15–16, 19–20;
Matthew 5:17–19

"Do not think that I have come to abolish the law
or the prophets; I have come not to abolish but to
fulfill."

—Matthew 5:17

Francis holds his followers to the highest standards of
the Gospel. Like the great St. Augustine, who said,
"Love and do what you will," Francis knows that if the
Lesser Brothers strive for the ideal, they will be unlikely
to break the more basic commandments.

And this is my advice, my counsel, and my earnest
plea to my friars in our Lord Jesus Christ that,
when they travel about the world, they should
not be quarrelsome or take part in disputes with
words (see 2 Timothy 2:14) or criticize others; but
they should be gentle, peaceful, and unassuming,
courteous and humble, speaking respectfully to
everyone, as is expected of them…. Whatever
house they enter, they should first say, "Peace to

this house" (Luke 10:5), and in the words of the Gospel they may eat what is set before them (Luke 10:8).

Whenever he preached, Francis first prayed for peace for his listeners, saying: "The Lord give you peace." He always most devoutly announced peace to men and women, to all he met and overtook. For this reason many who had hated peace and had hated also salvation embraced peace, through the co-operation of the Lord, with all their heart and were made children of peace and seekers after eternal salvation.

A peaceful attitude can go a long way toward living the message of the Gospel. If we think (and pray) before we speak or act, we will save ourselves and others a great deal of misunderstanding and heartache.

Prayer

Where there is Love and Wisdom, there is neither Fear nor Ignorance.

Where there is Patience and Humility, there is neither Anger nor Annoyance.

Amen.

Thursday of the Third Week of Lent
NOTHING TO DEFEND

Jeremiah 7:23–28; Psalm 95:1–2, 6–7, 8–9;
Luke 11:14–23

"Every kingdom divided against itself becomes a desert, and house falls on house."

—Luke 11:17

At the time of Francis, Italy was not a united nation, but numerous city-states, each with its own ruler and militia. Francis was well-acquainted with constantly warring factions, often backed by one Church official or another. He understood the futility of relying on human strength and weapons.

The brothers often asked the advice of the Bishop, who received Francis with kindness, but said: "It seems to me that it is very hard and difficult to possess nothing in the world." To this blessed Francis replied: "My Lord, if we had any possessions we should also be forced to have arms to protect them, since possessions are a cause of disputes and strife, and in many ways we should be hindered from loving God and our neighbor.

Therefore in this life we wish to have no temporal possessions."

The Bishop was greatly pleased by these words of God's servant; and indeed Francis despised all passing things, especially money, so much that he laid the greatest stress on holy poverty and insisted that the brothers should be most careful to avoid money.

We have so much in our lives that we feel we need to defend. It can lead us to live in constant fear. If we have nothing to defend, we have room to discover the providence and the peace that relying on God alone brings to our lives.

Prayer

Holy Wisdom puts Satan
and all his wiles to shame.
Amen.

Friday of the Third Week of Lent
PERFECT JOY
Hosea 14:2–10; Psalm 8:6c–8a, 8bc–9,
10–11ab, 14, 17; Mark 12:28b–34

"Which commandment is the first of all?"
—Mark 12 :28

One of the best stories about St. Francis is his explanation to Brother Leo about "perfect joy."

One winter day St. Francis was coming to St. Mary of the Angels from Perugia with Brother Leo, and the bitter cold made them suffer keenly. St. Francis…said: "Brother Leo, even if the Friars Minor in every country give a great example of holiness and integrity and good edification, nevertheless write down and note carefully that perfect joy is not in that."

…And going on a bit farther, St. Francis called again strongly: "Brother Leo, even if a Friar Minor could preach so well that he should convert all infidels to the faith of Christ, write that perfect joy is not there."

Now when he had been talking this way for a distance of two miles, Brother Leo in great amazement asked him: "Father, I beg you in God's name to tell me where perfect joy is."

And St. Francis replied: "When we come to St. Mary of the Angels, soaked by the rain and frozen by the cold, all soiled with mud and suffering from hunger, and we ring at the gate of the Place and the brother porter comes and says angrily: 'Who are you?' And we say: 'We are two of your brothers.' And he contradicts us, saying: 'You are not telling the truth. Rather you are two rascals who go around deceiving people and stealing what they give to the poor. Go away!'…and if we can bear it patiently and take the insults with joy and love in our hearts, oh, Brother Leo, write that perfect joy is there!"

Francis discovered the hidden secret to inner peace: Don't react. It doesn't make the insults OK. But it does keep us from being consumed by our own anger.

Prayer
You are joy and gladness.
You are justice and moderation. Amen.

Saturday of the Third Week of Lent
HOLY HUMILITY
Hosea 6:1–6; Psalm 51:3–4, 18–19, 20–21ab;
Luke 18:9–14

"He also told this parable to some who trusted in themselves that they were righteous and regarded others with contempt."

—Luke 18:9

Humility is one of the most enduring characteristics of Francis's life and attitudes. It's the foundation of his love for Lady Poverty. It makes possible his commitment to peace. And he recognizes, as Jesus does in the Gospels, that the most difficult obstacle to overcome in realizing the kingdom of God are those people who don't admit to their own sinfulness.

One day, he sought out a place of prayer… frequently repeating this word: O God, be merciful to me the sinner. Little by little a certain unspeakable joy and very great sweetness began to flood his innermost heart. He began also to stand aloof from himself, and, as his feelings were checked and the darkness that had gathered in his heart because of his fear of sin dispelled, there was poured into him a certainty that all his sins had been forgiven and a confidence of his restoration to grace was given him. He was then caught up above himself, and absorbed in a certain light; the capacity of his mind was enlarged and he could see clearly what was to come to pass. When this sweetness finally passed, along with the light, renewed in spirit, he seemed changed into another man.

True humility is knowing so well who we are in God's loving sight that nothing anyone says or does can shake us.

Prayer

Hail, Queen Wisdom!

The Lord save you, with your sister, pure, holy Simplicity.

Lady Holy Poverty,

God keep you, with your sister, holy Humility.

Amen.

Fourth Sunday of Lent
LEARNING TO SEE

Year A: 1 Samuel 16:1b, 6–7, 10–13; Psalm 23:1–3a, 3b–4, 5, 6; Ephesians 5:8–14; John 9:1–41

Year B: 2 Chronicles 36:14–16, 19–23; Psalm 137:1–2, 3, 4–5, 6; Ephesians 2:4–10; John 3:14–21

Year C: Joshua 5:9a, 10–12; Psalm 34:2–3, 4–5, 6–7; 2 Corinthians 5:17–21; Luke 15:1–3, 11–32

"Jesus answered, 'Neither this man nor his parents sinned; he was born blind so that God's works might be revealed in him.'"

—John 9:3

Just as spiritual blindness can be far more devastating than the loss of physical sight, so having our vision of God's grace restored can bring healing far beyond the physical. We see hope where once we knew only despair, and more than that we see new ways to communicate that hope to others. We see light instead of darkness, and in that light we discover a side of ourselves that we thought we had lost. We look with new eyes on the people around us and see how they, too, are children of God.

One of Francis's greatest works is his "Canticle of the Creatures." Francis wrote it late in his life. He was nearly blind from an eye disease acquired on his missionary travels. He could no longer see any of the natural delights that he had enjoyed throughout his life. In the midst of darkness and suffering, he praised light and joy. The paradox of our Christian life will always be that only through death do we obtain eternal life. If we begin with that belief as our firm foundation, we can follow Christ and his saints in turning the sadness and struggles of our lives into a means of praising God in our hearts, even if our minds take a little longer to understand.

Prayer

Most high, all-powerful, all good, Lord!
All praise is yours, all glory, all honour
And all blessing.
Amen.

Monday of the Fourth Week of Lent
SIGNS AND WONDERS
Isaiah 65:17–21; Psalm 30:2, 4, 5–6, 11–12a, 13b;
John 4:43–54

"Unless you see signs and wonders you will not believe."

—John 4:48

Francis strenuously denied the suggestions that he was a saint. He kept hidden the marks of the stigmata. He refused to let people attribute miracles to him. He knew, as Jesus did, the human desire for signs and wonders, for the extraordinary and the marvelous. And they both knew that it was easy for people to get stuck there.

St. Bonaventure's *Major Life of St. Francis* shows us that after Francis's death, the signs of his holiness could no longer be hidden.

> After his death the Lord made the truth of them still more manifest through miracles which occurred in different parts of the world. These miracles touched the hearts of many persons who had not rightly judged and appreciated the servant of God during his life time, and had doubted

about the stigmata. Their doubt was changed into such faith and certainty that many who had formerly decried the servant of God were moved through the Lord to accept the truth and they became fervent in praising him and in spreading his fame and teaching.

We rejoice in the great things that Francis did during his lifetime and continues to do in the communion of saints. But those who spend time meditating on the words of Francis can also feel a twinge of regret for the hiddenness and humility he so valued during his lifetime. It serves as a reminder not to desire fame and fortune but to seek, as Francis did, only the grace of God.

Prayer

All praise be yours, my Lord, through all that you have made,

And first my lord Brother Sun,

Who brings the day; and light you give to us through him.

How beautiful is he, how radiant in all his splendour!

Amen.

Tuesday of the Fourth Week of Lent
DO WE LIKE COMPLAINING?
Ezekiel 47:1–9, 12; Psalm 46:2–3, 5–6, 8–9;
John 5:1–3a, 5–16

"I have no one to put me into the pool."

—John 5:6

Today's Gospel tells us that the man by the pool of Bethesda has been ill for thirty-eight years. He sounds a bit querulous as he lies there waiting for someone to take care of his problems. And when Jesus does heal him and tells him to sin no more, he tells the authorities where to find Jesus.

Not everyone wants to be well. Too often we become invested in our own weakness, our own sickness. It seems we would rather complain than deal with the responsibility of being healed. It can take a great deal of reflection, prayer, and good counsel to overcome this inertia.

One of the legends associated with St. Francis tells of a vineyard near a church in the Rieti valley. Francis was staying there while being treated for eye problems. So many people came to visit him that the vineyard was trampled. The priest complained that he would not get the small yield of grapes on which he relied for his household wine each year. Francis assured him that he would harvest at least twenty loads of grapes that year instead of the usual thirteen.

What's more interesting than the miracle that Francis promised (and which did in fact occur) is what Francis said to the priest: "Cease despairing. Don't trouble anyone any more with your complaints. Have confidence in the Lord and in my words."

How often do we really place our trust in the Lord? Complaining can become a habit and it can soon burden our spirits—and our friends. When we're going through tough times, some amount of struggle and grief is to be expected. But as people of faith, we know that at some point we need to let go of the grieving and move forward with grace.

Prayer

Where there is Mercy and Prudence, there is neither Excess nor Harshness.

Amen.

Wednesday of the Fourth Week of Lent
THE VIRTUE OF WORK
Isaiah 49:8–15; Psalm 145:8–9, 13cd–14, 17–18;
John 5:17–30

"My Father is still working, and I also am working."

—John 5:17

Francis not only encouraged his brothers to work; he preferred that they be about manual labor—concrete, physical actions that could be clearly seen and rightly interpreted. His Rule of 1221 instructed:

> The friars who have a trade should work at it, provided that it is no obstacle to their spiritual progress and can be practised without scandal. The Psalmist tells us, You shall eat the fruit of your handiwork; happy shall you be, and favoured (127:2); and St. Paul adds, If any man will not work, neither let him eat (2 Thessalonians 3:10). Everyone should remain at the trade and in the position in which he was called. In payment they may accept anything they need, except money. If necessary, they can go for alms like the rest of the

friars. They are allowed to have the tools which they need for their trade.

All the friars must work hard doing good, as it has been said, "Always be doing something worthwhile; then the devil will always find you busy" and, "Idleness is the enemy of the soul." And so those who serve God should be always busy praying or doing good.

More and more people work at occupations that make few physical demands. While there will always be jobs that involve manual labor, not everyone can enjoy the satisfaction that comes with seeing a concrete result from physical work. Often our hobbies reveal that we need to do things with our hands, we need to be active, we need to use our bodies as well as our minds.

To what good work can you lend your hands today?

Prayer

All praise be yours, my Lord, through Brothers Wind and Air,
And fair and stormy, all the weather's moods,
By which you cherish all that you have made.
Amen.

Thursday of the Fourth Week of Lent
HOW DO OTHERS SEE US?
Exodus 32:7–14; Psalm 106:19–20, 21–22, 23;
John 5:31–47

"How can you believe when you accept glory from
one another and do not seek the glory that comes
from the one who alone is God?"

—John 5:44

Francis was concerned with the impression that he
made on those around him. In his early life, he wanted
to be noticed for his fine clothes, courtly manners,
and military prowess. After his conversion, he was
concerned that people might think him a hypocrite for
preaching absolute poverty and then receiving gifts or
small luxuries from his admirers.

When a medical condition required that Francis wear
a softer material (fox skin) next to his body, Francis said:

If you want me to permit this under my tunic,
then have a piece of the same size attached to the
outside, which, sewn on the outside, will show
men that there is a skin hidden inside too.

Does our outward appearance accurately portray our inner attitude? In some measure, the disciplines of Lent—prayer, fasting, almsgiving—help us to bring these two closer together. But we need to be mindful that we don't take this too far. If we find ourselves doing these things for the praise we might get from others for our holiness, it's time to step back and examine our motives and priorities. What we are is more important than what we seem to be.

Prayer

All praise be yours, my Lord,
through those who grant pardon for love of you;
through those who endure Sickness and trial.
Amen.

Friday of the Fourth Week of Lent
THE KINGDOM IS RIGHT HERE
Wisdom 2:1a, 12–22; Psalm 34:17–18, 19–20, 21, 23;
John 7:1–2, 10, 25–30

"You know me, and you know where I am from."
—John 7:28

Jesus is responding to some of the Jews saying that "When the Christ comes, no one will know where he is from." This becomes an issue again and again throughout the Gospels. We like to think that the origins of our holy people are shrouded in mystery, in part because it allows us to set them apart as different from us. This gives us a built-in reason not to emulate them too closely. The incarnation turns this upside down. Suddenly we discover that our God became one of us, precisely to show us how to live.

Many of our saints are identified by their place of origin. In some cases this is to differentiate them from other saints who share the same name. In others, it's because of a local veneration that developed either during or after their lifetimes.

St. Francis of Assisi is one of those saints identified with a particular place. The town in which he was born and where he lived his entire life shaped the way he viewed the world, the places he discovered God's presence, his awareness of the people he served. In visiting Assisi, pilgrims come to understand more about Francis than they could in any other way.

Like Jesus of Nazareth, Francis of Assisi was able to accomplish a great deal in a small, somewhat obscure village. They know that proximity to power, to wealth, to a thriving metropolis doesn't guarantee the kind of impact they seek to have on the world.

We can take comfort in this, especially if we ourselves aren't particularly well-placed. We can also be challenged by it. Suddenly we have no excuse not to do what we can in whatever place we find ourselves. We don't need to move to a big city—or to mission territory. The kingdom of God is in our midst in all places and at all times. All we need to do is acknowledge it and spread that awareness to others through lives faithful to the Gospel.

Prayer

Each and every virtue puts vice and sin to shame. Amen.

Saturday of the Fourth Week of Lent

LIMITATIONS

Jeremiah 11:18–20; Psalm 7:2–3, 9bc–10, 11–12;
John 7:40–53

"But some asked, 'Surely the Messiah does not come from Galilee, does he?'"

—John 7:40

We know that, although he spent much time in Assisi, Francis and his companions also traveled around the country a bit. On a few occasions they traveled all the way to Rome, the home of the pope and the Vatican, the heart of the Catholic Church. Francis, as always, brought his own perspective to these trips.

At this time he happened to go to Rome on pilgrimage, and in the church of Saint Peter he noticed that many people left what seemed to him very inadequate offerings. He said to himself: "Surely, the greatest honor is due to the Prince of the Apostles; how then can some folk leave such meagre alms in the church where his body rests?" Full of fervor he took a handful of money from his purse and threw it in through a grating in the altar; the coins made such a clatter that those present heard it and were greatly astonished at such munificence.

Francis then left the church, and on the steps before the entrance a number of beggars were asking for money from those who came and went. Francis quietly borrowed the clothes of one of these beggars, changing into them from his own; and, dressed in rags, he stood on the steps with the others, asking for alms…

There's something attractive about being able to reinvent ourselves. It's difficult, though not impossible, to do this if we stay in the same place with the same people all our lives. Perhaps the lesson we can learn from Francis is not to let ourselves be limited by what people might think they know about us.

Prayer

All praise be yours, my Lord, through Brother Fire,
Through whom you brighten up the night.
Amen.

Fifth Sunday of Lent
SISTER DEATH

Year A: Ezekiel 37:12–14; Psalm 130:1–2, 3–4, 5–6, 7–8;
Romans 8:8–11; John 11:1–45
Year B: Jeremiah 31:31–34; Psalm 51: 3–4, 12–13, 14–15;
Hebrews 5:7–9; John 12:20–33
Year C: Isaiah 43:16–21; Psalm 126:1–2a, 2b–3, 4–5, 6;
Philippians 3:8–14; John 8:1–11

"Martha said to him, 'I know that he will rise again in the resurrection on the last day.' Jesus said to her, 'I am the resurrection and the life.'"
—John 11:24–25

Death always startles us with its suddenness, its finality. Even when a loved one has been sick for a long time and death comes as a relief for both the sufferer and those left behind, the initial reaction is one of shock. In cases of sudden, accidental death, this reaction is magnified. We who believe in the resurrection are no less likely to experience this human reaction.

We resonate with Mary's response to Jesus about her belief in the resurrection at the end of time. Our minds and our faith tell us one thing, but our hearts and our bodies often balk at the appearance of separation and loss that for a time is all too real and unavoidable. Like so much of our spiritual lives, we have to learn to live with this paradox.

We see it differently at different times in our life. When we're young, death is an infrequent and scary interruption of life. When we're old, we sometimes feel like we've seen too much death over the course of a long life, and it seems almost unbearable in its familiarity.

The promise of resurrection at the heart of our faith allows us to celebrate our loved ones even in their passing, because we know that life, not death, is the final reality.

The final verse of St. Francis's "Canticle of the Creatures" praises bodily death. Scholars tell us that Francis added these words shortly before his own death, after Brother Leo and Brother Angelo had sung the Canticle at his request. Thomas of Celano tells us that Francis's last words were, "Welcome, my Sister Death."

Prayer

All praise be yours, my Lord, through Sister Death,
From whose embrace no mortal can escape.
Amen.

Monday of the Fifth Week of Lent
GREAT COMPASSION
Daniel 13:1–9, 15–17, 19–30, 33–62;
Psalm 23:1–3a, 3b–4, 5, 6; John 8:1–11

"Neither do I condemn you."

—John 8:11

While Francis was on his journey to visit the sultan, he stayed overnight in an inn, where he was approached by a prostitute.

St. Francis answered her: "If you wish me to do what you want, you must also do what I want." "I agree," she said. "So let's go and prepare a bed." And she led him toward a room. But St. Francis said to her: "Come with me, and I will show you a very beautiful bed." And he led her to a very large fire that was burning in that house at that time. And in fervor of spirit he stripped himself naked and threw himself down on the fire in the fireplace as on a bed. And he called to her, saying: "Undress and come quickly and enjoy this splendid, flowery, and wonderful bed, because you must be here if you wish to obey me!" And he remained there for a long time with a joyful face, resting on the fire-place as though on flowers, but the fire did not burn or singe him.

The roaring fire can easily be seen as the fires of lust and temptation that Francis, in his joyful commitment to his Lord, has managed to overcome. We can imagine that there were others, like the woman in this story, who were inspired by Francis's chastity.

As we approach the final week of Lent, the spiritual stakes are high. At some point in our journey, we each are called to spend time alone with Jesus, hearing him speak to us the words he spoke to the woman in today's Gospel: "Neither do I condemn you. Go and from now on do not sin anymore."

Prayer

Holy Love puts to shame
all the temptations of the devil
and the flesh
and all natural fear.
Amen.

Tuesday of the Fifth Week of Lent
THE SIGN OF THE CROSS
Numbers 21:4–9; Psalm 102:2–3, 16–18, 19–21;
John 8:21–30

"When you have lifted up the Son of Man, then you will realize that I am he, and that I do nothing on my own…"

—John 8:28

Francis prayed continually to be identified with the crucified Christ. His efforts throughout his life to conform himself to the Gospel eventually resulted in a visible manifestation of that prayer.

Two years before Francis gave his soul back to heaven, while he was living in the hermitage which was called Alverna, after the place on which it stood, he saw in the vision of God a man standing above him, like a seraph with six wings, his hands extended and his feet joined together and fixed to a cross. Two of the wings were extended above his head, two were extended as if for flight, and two were wrapped around the whole body…. [T]he fact that the seraph was fixed to a cross and the sharpness of his suffering filled Francis with fear…. [W]hile he was thus unable to come to any understanding of it and the strangeness of the vision perplexed his heart, the marks of the nails began to appear in his hands and feet, just as he had seen them a little before in the crucified man above him…. Furthermore, his right side was as though it had been pierced by a lance.

Our Lenten journey isn't likely to lead to this kind of spiritual experience. But we can take away from it something of the absorbing love Francis had for God. We can pray that in our own way we will increase our love for God and come to see signs of that love in the relationships we have with one another.

Prayer

You are holy, Lord, the only God, and your deeds are wonderful.

You are strong. You are great.

You are the Most High, You are almighty.

You, holy Father, are King of heaven and earth.

Amen.

Wednesday of the Fifth Week of Lent
TRUE DISCIPLES
Daniel 3:14–20, 91–92, 95; Daniel 3:52, 53,
54, 55, 56; John 8:31–42

"If you continue in my word, you are truly my disciples; and you will know the truth, and the truth will make you free."

—John 8:31–32

In modeling his life on the Gospels, Francis hoped that people would see in him and in the Lesser Brothers an example of what they, too, could achieve if they would only follow Jesus. Francis had a profound ability to translate what many saw as only sacred words to be read at Mass into a way of life that could be adapted to any place and time.

People now saw how the brothers rejoiced in the midst of trials and tribulation; how zealous they were in prayer; and how they did not accept money like other people, nor keep it when it was given them; and how they really loved one another. Seeing all this, many became convinced that the brothers were true disciples of Jesus Christ; and with remorse in their hearts they came to ask the brothers pardon for having previously injured and insulted them. The brothers forgave them gladly, saying: "The Lord forgive you," and gently admonished them concerning their salvation…. When they were all together, joy filled their hearts, and they no longer remembered past injuries.

How do we, in our own lives, set an example for the people around us? This will always be a more powerful way of sharing the good news than anything we could say.

Prayer

Lord, make me an instrument of your peace.
Where there is hatred, let me sow love.
Where there is injury, pardon.
Where there is doubt, faith.
Where there is despair, hope.
Where there is darkness, light.
Where there is sadness, joy.
Amen.

Thursday of the Fifth Week of Lent
WHAT IS OURS?
Genesis 17:3–9; Psalm 105:4–5, 6–7, 8–9;
John 8:51–59

"Are you greater than our father Abraham?"

—John 8:53

Francis wanted to make sure that his brothers under-stood that any glory they might experience always reflected more on God's goodness than on any merit of their own.

We…have nothing of our own, except our vices and sins. And so we should be glad when we fall into various trials (James 1:2), and when we suffer anguish of soul or body, or affliction of any kind in this world, for the sake of life eternal. We must all be on our guard against pride and empty boasting and beware of worldly or natural wisdom…. It was about people like this that our Lord said, Amen I say to you, they have received their reward (Matthew 6:2). The spirit of God, on the other hand, inspires us to mortify and despise our lower nature and regard it as a source of shame, worthless and of no value. Humility, patience, perfect simplicity, and true peace of heart are all its aim, but above everything else it desires the fear of God, the divine wisdom and the divine love of the Father, Son, and Holy Spirit.

These can be hard words to hear, harder still to do. But this has been the core of the message throughout this holy season of Lent. The Gospel and the Rule of Francis are both utterly simple as read, but profoundly life-changing as lived. They are the source of lifelong conversion, of coming ever closer to our God. One of the last things Francis said to his followers was, "I have done what is mine to do. May the Lord teach you what is yours."

Prayer
You are love, You are wisdom.
You are humility, You are endurance.
You are rest, You are peace.
Amen.

Friday of the Fifth Week of Lent
PRAISING GOD
Jeremiah 20:10–13; Psalm 18:2–3a, 3bc–4,
5–6, 7; John 10:31–42

"It is not for a good work that we are going to stone you, but for blasphemy."

—John 10:33

Francis understood that the way to imitate Jesus was by doing the good works that he had done, but there was also a mystical dimension to that identification. He wasn't simply looking for a better way to live; he was looking for a way to identify completely with God and in so doing give God the most complete praise possible.

Blessed Francis also warned his brothers never to judge or criticize those who live in luxury, eat fastidiously, and indulge in superfluous and splendid clothes; God, he said, is their Lord and ours; he has the power to call them to himself and to justify them. He insisted that the friars should reverence such men as their brothers and masters, and they are indeed brothers since they are children of the same Creator; while they are our masters since they help the good to do penance by giving them what is necessary to the body. To this blessed Francis added: "The general behavior of the friars among people must be such that all who see or hear them may be drawn to glorify our heavenly Father and to praise him devoutly."

Francis is often admired by people who have no interest in God, who do not believe in an afterlife, who believe that the only good to be done is here on earth. Those of us who profess the Christian faith know that there's more to life than this limited time on earth.

Francis and Jesus keep us from over-spiritualizing our faith. They keep us attentive to the very human needs of the poor and least ones in our midst. But they also remind us again and again not to lose sight of the big picture, that which gives true meaning to all our lives.

Prayer

You are our protector,
You are our guardian and defender.
You are courage.
You are our haven and our hope.
Amen.

Saturday of the Fifth Week of Lent
WORLDLY POWER
Ezekiel 37:21–28; Jeremiah 31:10, 11–12, 13;
John 11:45–57

"If we let him go on like this, everyone will believe
in him, and the Romans will come and destroy
both our holy place and our nation."

—John 11:48

Even after his conversion, Francis retains something
of his antipathy for the Perugians, historical enemies
of Assisi and the faction that imprisoned him in his
fighting days:

Coming therefore to Perugia, he began to preach
to the people who had gathered about; but when
some knights rode up on their horses, as is their
custom, and crossing their weapons in a military
exercise, interfered with his words, the saint turned
toward them and sighing, said: "O miserable folly
of wretched men who do not consider nor fear
the judgment of God! But listen to what the Lord
announces to you through me, poor little one. The
Lord," he said, "has exalted you above all others

around you; for this reason you should be kinder to your neighbors and you should live in a way more pleasing to God. But, ungrateful for God's grace, you attack your neighbors with arms, kill and plunder them. I say to you: this will not go unpunished; but, for your greater punishment, God will cause you to fall into civil war, so that one will rise against the other in mutual sedition. Wrath will teach you, for kindness has not taught you."

The point of this story is not that God punishes our temporal enemies. Rather, it shows the logical conclusion of those who steadfastly refuse to adopt a life of peace, kindness, love of God and neighbor. It also suggests that trying to wield worldly, political power will nearly always end in disaster.

Prayer

Where there is the Fear of God to guard the dwelling, there no enemy can enter.

Amen.

Palm Sunday of the Lord's Passion
THE CROSS IS BEFORE US
Procession Gospel:
Year A: Matthew 21:1–11; Year B: Mark 11:1–10 or
John 12:12–16; Year C: Luke 19:28–40
First Reading, Psalm, Second Reading:
Year A, B, C: Isaiah 50:4–7; Psalm 22:8–9, 17–18, 19–20,
23–24; Philippians 2:6–11
Gospel:
Year A: Matthew 26:14—27:66; Year B: Mark 14:1—
15:47; Year C: Luke 22:14—23:56

"They took branches of palm trees and went out
to meet him."

—John 12:13

The cross is before us now with its wordless challenge to
love beyond death. Take some time this week to think
about events in your own life that have given you an
experience of Jesus's command to pick up your cross
and follow him.

St. Clare was one of the first followers of St. Francis.
Raised in a wealthy family, whose home overlooked
the piazza of Assisi's cathedral, she must have heard

Francis preaching often. Moved by his radical message of Gospel poverty, she made up her mind to follow him and his companions.

On the night of Palm Sunday in 1212 she left her home and walked through the darkened streets to the gate that led to her new life. It can be difficult for us to imagine what a drastic decision this was for Clare.

We, too, are called to move out of our comfort zones, to take steps to follow the Gospel more radically in our lives. They might be small steps or they might be as drastic as Clare leaving home to work among the poor and the lepers. What these steps have in common is faith that God is leading us on this journey. And just as Francis and his brothers welcomed Clare, the communion of saints encourages us on our way.

Prayer

Most High, Glorious God,
bring light to the darkness of my heart,
give me right faith, certain hope, and perfect charity.
Lord, give me insight and wisdom
so I might always discern
your holy and true will.
Amen.

Monday of Holy Week
TRUE CONCERN FOR THE POOR
Isaiah 42:1–7; Psalm 27:1, 2, 3, 13–14; John 12:1–11

"Why was this perfume not sold for three hundred denarii and the money given to the poor?"
—John 12:5

Judas's question in today's Gospel can generate nearly endless debate about the role of almsgiving and charity in the Christian life. Francis seems to have been acutely aware of the deceptions and subterfuges of some who wanted to follow him. A story is told by several of his biographers of a man known as Brother Fly.

After Francis had preached…a certain man came humbly asking to be admitted into the order. The saint said to him: "If you wish to be joined with the poor, first distribute your possessions to the poor of the world." When he heard this, the man left, and, impelled by a carnal love, he distributed his goods to his relatives and gave nothing to the poor. It happened that when he came back and told the saint of his generous liberality, the father laughed at him and said: "Go on your way, brother fly, for you have not yet left your home and your relatives. You gave your goods to your relatives and you have defrauded the poor; you are not worthy to be numbered among the holy poor. You have begun with the flesh, you have laid an unsound foundation on which to build a spiritual structure." That carnal man returned to his own and got back his goods which he did not want to give to the poor and for that reason he abandoned very quickly his virtuous purpose.

The tension between material possessions and the spiritual life has always been part of religious life. We see it in our own religious institutions and in our own lives.

Francis knew the many dangers of money. If we listen to his cautions and strive to live his ideals, we can rest assured that we won't go too far off the path.

Prayer

All praise be yours, my Lord, through Sister Water,
So useful, lowly, precious and pure.
Amen.

Tuesday of Holy Week
Isaiah 49:1–6; Psalm 71:1–2, 3–4a, 5–6ab, 15, 17;
John 13:21–33, 36–38

"Very truly, I tell you, one of you will betray me."
—John 13:21

In John's Gospel, Jesus knows what is happening at all times. The events are part of a greater plan. He knows that he will be betrayed and he knows who his betrayer is. Yesterday we heard Judas challenge him over the jar of ointment used to anoint him. Today Jesus tells Judas to be about his errand. In both instances, John reminds his readers that Judas was the keeper of the community's money.

We have seen throughout the accounts of Francis's life and woven into his writings a deep distrust of money. He made it a part of the rule of life for his companions that they not handle money, that they treat it with contempt, that they regard it as having little more value than dust or dung.

While this might seem extreme to us today, we can also see the way the Gospels also suggest that there is something about money that turns people from the good. Judas, we are told elsewhere, agrees to betray Jesus for thirty pieces of silver, money he later flings back at the temple priests. And Jesus himself drives the moneychangers from the temple.

In this holiest of weeks, we are challenged more than ever to think about our own relationship with money and material goods. Are we in danger of letting it come between ourselves and our God or ourselves and our loved ones? Money questions can ruin relationships, inner peace, spiritual well-being. We like to think we can separate our finances and our prayer lives. Jesus and Francis remind us that we can't, that we have to wrestle with these questions again and again. Is that where our confrontation with the cross hits home?

Prayer

Lady Holy Love, God keep you,
with your sister, holy Obedience.
Amen.

Wednesday of Holy Week
BETRAYAL
Isaiah 50:4–9a; Psalm 69:8–10, 21–22, 31, 33–34;
Matthew 26:14–25

"Surely not I, Lord?"

—Matthew 26:22

Yesterday we heard John's account of the betrayal by Judas. Today we hear the same story from Matthew's Gospel. The first three days of Holy Week focus almost exclusively on the act of betrayal by one of Jesus's twelve closest followers.

Matthew tells us that the Twelve were deeply distressed by Jesus's prediction of betrayal. They each questioned him, saying, "Surely it is not I, Lord?" We can see in their question that each one may have suspected that he might be capable of it, that his faith wasn't as strong as it might be.

I suspect they were also horrified because, like us, they had all known betrayal at one time or another in their lives. It's something that strikes at the heart of relationships, at the trust that we rely on to keep us in community and family.

Do we always end up betraying Jesus at some point? We are all sinners. We all need salvation, again and again and again. And so we come to the paschal mystery, the suffering, death, and resurrection of Jesus. Francis reminds us:

Remember the words of our Lord, Love your enemies, do good to those who hate you (Matthew 5:44). Our Lord Jesus Christ himself, in whose footsteps we must follow (see 1 Peter 2:21), called the man who betrayed him his friend, and gave himself up of his own accord to his executioners. Therefore, our friends are those who for no reason cause us trouble and suffering, shame or injury, pain or torture, even martyrdom and death. It is these we must love, and love very much, because for all they do to us we are given eternal life.

Prayer

All praise be yours, my Lord,
through Sister Moon and Stars;
In the heavens you have made them, bright
And precious and fair.
Amen.

Easter Triduum: Holy Thursday
EUCHARIST

Exodus 12:1–8, 11–14; Psalm 116:12–13, 15–16, 17–18; 1
Corinthians 11:23–26; John 13:1–5

"I received from the Lord what I also handed on
to you."

—1 Corinthians 11:23

St. Francis was absolutely devoted to the Eucharist.
It's one of the reasons he was so concerned about
rebuilding and cleaning local churches, making them
suitable homes for the Eucharist.

Thomas of Celano tells us that concerned citizens
brought St. Francis to their parish priest who was
living in sin; they wanted the saint to reprimand him
and condemn his sinful way of life. Instead, St. Francis
knelt, took the priest's hands and said, "I know not
whether this priest is sinful. I only know that these
hands, and these hands alone, make present upon the
altar my Lord and Savior Jesus Christ."

Francis's respect for the clergy was based on the
priest's power to change bread and wine into the Body
and Blood of Christ, "in whom all things in heaven and

on earth are made peaceful and are reconciled to God the Almighty."

The Church of his day was no stranger to scandal and corruption. He reminds us that there's more to the Church than the human insititution, that the Holy Spirit continues to guide the Church throughout history, even when all appearances seem to the contrary.

Today's Gospel account of Jesus washing the disciples' feet offers an antitdote to the problems our human Church encounters. Francis takes this to heart in his *Admonitions* when he says:

> I did not come to be served but to serve (Matthew 20:28), our Lord tells us. Those who are put in charge of others should be no prouder of their office than if they had been appointed to wash the feet of their confreres. They should be no more upset at the loss of their authority than they would be if they were deprived of the task of washing feet. The more they are upset, the greater the risk they incur to their souls.

Prayer
Of you, Most High, he bears the likeness.
Amen.

Easter Triduum: Good Friday
"BY YOUR HOLY CROSS"
Isaiah 52:13—53:12; Psalm 31:2, 6, 12–13, 15–16, 17, 25;
Hebrews 4:14–16; 5:7–9; John 18:1—19:42

"One of the soldiers pierced his side with a spear,
and at once blood and water came out."

—John 19:34

The Passion According to St. John is always read on Good Friday. It gives us a perspective on the death of Jesus that reminds us that it wasn't simply a tragic occurrence in the life of a good man. It was the culmination of the earthly ministry of the Son of God, his hour of glorification, that moment when heaven and earth are joined and the life of Christ became the ongoing life of the Church.

For St. Francis, meditating on the Passion was not some medieval exercise in masochism but a means of uniting himself completely to the sacrifice of Christ on the cross, a way of living so thoroughly into the mystery of Christ that he was able to lead others into this mystery.

He wrote in his *Testament*:

And God inspired me with such faith in his churches that I used to pray with all simplicity, saying, "We adore you, Lord Jesus Christ, here and in all your churches in the whole world, and we bless you, because by your holy cross you have redeemed the world."

Francis's conversion began with his prayer before the cross of the ruined chapel of San Damiano and culminated in his experience of the stigmata on Mount La Verna. As we journey with him, he brings us always to the cross and to Christ.

Prayer

Happy those [Death] finds doing your will!
The second death can do no harm to them.
Praise and bless my Lord, and give him thanks,
And serve him with great humility.
Amen.

Easter Triduum:
Holy Saturday / Easter Vigil
DEAD TO SIN
The Vigil offers a choice of eight readings from the Old Testament, with psalm responses.

Exodus 14:15—15:1 must always be used.
Romans 6:3–11; Psalm 118:1–2, 16–17, 22–23
Gospel: Year A: Matthew 28:1–10; Year B: Mark 16:1–7;
Year C: Luke 24:1–12

"So you also must consider yourselves dead to sin and alive to God in Christ Jesus."

—Romans 6:11

Francis described his life before his conversion as "When I was in sin." St. Paul's Letter to the Romans, a part of which is always read at the Easter Vigil, reminds us that we died with Christ in our baptism and so will rise with him in the resurrection.

We have journeyed through this Lent with St. Francis, reflecting with him on the cross of Christ, the Gospel call to poverty, care for the poor, the dangers and temptations that can beset us even when we're striving to live a good and holy life. As we come now to the celebration of Easter, we recall that one of the hallmarks of Francis's life was a deep joy in the love of Christ and the glories of creation:

> [St. Francis] was offered a present of a sheep at the Portiuncula and he accepted it gladly in his love of innocence and simplicity, two virtues which the image of a sheep naturally recalls. He exhorted the animal to give God praise and avoid offending the friars, and the sheep was careful to follow his instruction, just as if it realized the affection he had for it. If it was entering the church and heard the friars singing in the choir, it would go down on one knee spontaneously and bleat before the altar of our lady, the Mother of the Lamb, as if it were trying to greet her. At the elevation during Mass, it would bow profoundly on bended knees and reproach those who were not so devout by its very reverence, while giving the faithful an example of respect for the Blessed Sacrament.

Prayer

Most high, all-powerful, all good, Lord!
    No mortal lips are worthy to pronounce your name.
Amen.

Easter Triduum: Easter Sunday

"LET US BEGIN AGAIN"

Acts 10:34a, 37–43; Psalm 118:1–2, 16–17, 22–23;
Colossians 3:1–4 or 1 Corinthians 5:6b–8; John 20:1–9

"…he saw and believed."

—John 20:8

Easter is a beginning, not an ending. And this Easter story from Thomas of Celano reminds us that for Francis, the challenge to remain true to the Gospel was one that needed to be renewed again and again.

It happened one Easter that the brothers at the hermitage of Greccio prepared the table more carefully than they usually did with white linens and glassware. Coming down from his cell, the father came to the table and saw that it was placed high and decorated extravagantly. But he did not smile at the smiling table. Stealthily and little by little he retraced his steps, put on the hat of a poor man who was there, and taking a staff in his hand, he went outside. He waited outside at the door until the brothers began to eat; for they were in the habit of not waiting for him when he did not come at the signal. When they had begun to eat, this truly poor man cried out at the door; "For the love of the Lord God," he said, "give an alms to this poor, sick wanderer." The brothers answered: "Come in, man, for love of him whom you have invoked." He immediately entered and appeared before them as they were eating. But what astonishment, do you think, the beggar caused these inhabitants? The beggar was given a dish, and sitting alone, he put the dish in the ashes. "Now I am sitting as a Friar Minor should sit," he said.

Francis was like that other pilgrim alone in Jerusalem that day. But he made the hearts of the disciples burn when he spoke to them.

Prayer
Lord God, all good.
You are Good, all Good, supreme Good,
Lord God, living and true.
Amen.

ABOUT THE AUTHOR

Diane M. Houdek is the digital media editor for Franciscan Media, as well as author and editor of *Bringing Home the Word* and a senior editor of *Liberty+Vine*. She has written extensively for Franciscan Media, and is a past editor of *Scripture From Scratch* and *Weekday Homily Helps*.